GIFT

This Book Is A Gift

For: _____

From: _____

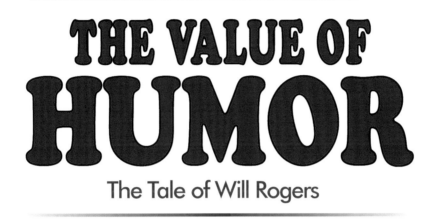

THE VALUE OF HUMOR

The Tale of Will Rogers

Timeless Values
In Entertaining Tales

For more information about The New ValueTales®:
1-800-515-0848

www.ValueTales.com

THE VALUE OF HUMOR

The Tale of Will Rogers

The New ValueTales® Series Created and Edited By
Spencer Johnson, M.D.

Based on
Original Text by
Spencer Johnson, M.D.
and
Original illustrations by
Steve Pileggi

ILLUSTRATED BY STEVE Pileggi

Candle
PUBLISHING

Candle
PUBLISHING
Better to light a candle
Than curse the darkness

The New ValueTale® Books Are Available At:
http://www.ValueTales.com
1 – 800 – 515 – 0848

Published in the United States of America by Candle Publishing.

Volume 6, Edition 1, *The New ValueTales® Series*

Published in 2007 under title: The Value of Humor: The Tale of Will Rogers.
First ed. published in 1977 under title: The ValueTale of Will Rogers: The Value of Humor.

Library of Congress Control Number: 2007929699

ISBN 978-1-934288-05-4

Personal Values; Historical Figures; Role Models; Juvenile Literature; Humor; Cowboy; Entertainment.

Manufactured in the United States of America.

WELCOME

This fictional tale is about Will Rogers, a real person who lived in Oklahoma, and traveled to many places in the world, in the 19th and 20th centuries.

This imaginative story is based on many historical events that really happened and it shows how useful the value of humor can be. More historical facts are found on page 64.

Now let's have fun with our story — *The Value of Humor: The Tale of Will Rogers …*

**O**NCE upon a time…

an interesting man, named Will Rogers, lived in a land called Oklahoma. He could see the funny side of things, and he liked to laugh.

Many people liked Will. They even built a statue of him.

Do you know why so many people liked him?

Well, it all began when Will was a little boy.

NEVER MET A MAN I DIDN'T LIKE

Will lived on his parents' ranch. Like most children, he liked to play and have fun, instead of doing his chores.

Sometimes he would let his pony swim in the cool stream. He would hang onto the pony's tail and laugh.

One day Will thought, "There's something I'd like to do that would be even more fun."

Will went to see Dan Walker, a cowboy who worked on the ranch, and asked, "Would you show me how to have fun with a lariat, your special kind of rope? I'd like to be the best roper in the world."

"Oh dear!" thought Will's mother when she heard this. "Whatever will become of Will? I'd like to see him grow up and become a minister and help people, but all he wants to do is twirl a rope."

Will began to spend a lot of time playing with his lariat. One day his father called, "Will, come here!"

"Uh, oh!" thought Will.

"You're playing with your rope when you should be doing your chores," scolded Will's father. "You're a good boy, Will," his father said kindly, "but you must do your work first, and *then* play."

Will felt sad because he had disappointed his father. He ran to finish his chores and then went off to be by himself.

Will sat quietly on a fence and tossed his lariat rope. He thought about what his father had said. "I wish I never got into trouble with my mom and dad," he thought. "I wish I always did the right thing."

As Will swung his lariat, he heard the humming sound that a twirling rope always makes as it spins through the air. Will used his imagination and pretended that the humming was the sound of his rope talking to him.

"Howdy, Will," the rope suddenly seemed to say. "I'm Larry — Larry Ett. I'd like to be your best friend."

Will laughed. "That's a funny name. But I'd like that, too."

He knew that his best friend was *himself.* Just like your best friend is *yourself.* He was really just talking to, and listening to himself. But it was more fun to think of his rope as his friend.

Larry Ett seemed to smile and say, "We can be partners. Now listen, partner, and I'll tell you something that might make you feel better."

What do you think Larry Ett said to Will?

"You could use a sense of humor," said Larry Ett, "which means you are smart enough to see what's funny in a situation and laugh at it. Then you would feel better."

"I don't feel like laughing," Will said. He went and sat on his bed.

Larry Ett smiled. "It's when you are taking things too seriously, and when you don't feel happy, that you need a sense of humor the most."

"When you learn to have a *great* sense of humor," Larry Ett revealed, "you can even laugh and learn from *any* situation you are in."

Will thought maybe Larry Ett had a good idea. But for now, he did not laugh. Maybe, he would think more about it later.

Before long, it was time for Will to go to school. As he rode with his dad from the ranch he thought, "I wonder what school will be like? I wonder what I can rope there with my lariat?"

"Uh, oh!" sighed Larry Ett. "Will's going to get into trouble again."

School wasn't anything like the ranch. There were no calves to rope. One day, during recess, Will was practicing with his rope. "I'll just toss my rope over that statue," he said.

"Will! Be careful!" cried Larry Ett.

Will did not know that the statue was not fastened to its base. "Oh, no!" he cried, as the statue toppled over and smashed into pieces.

The other boys laughed. But, Will began to worry, since his father would have to pay for the broken statue.

Determined to try to stay out of trouble, Will went off by himself to practice his roping. At least he thought he was alone.

But look carefully. Can you see who is coming around the corner of the school building?

What do you think is going to happen?

"Aaaagh!" Will's teacher choked. His face turned purple.

"Oh, no!" said Will. "I can't believe it. I'm in trouble again!" Will helped his teacher up and took off the rope. "I didn't see you. It was an accident."

"That's your last 'accident!'" roared the teacher. "You're expelled!"

Soon after his father learned that Will was still getting in trouble, he decided to send him to a very strict school — a military academy, where he hoped Will would be able learn self-discipline that might help him do well in life.

Larry Ett whispered, "Sometimes, it helps to look at your mistakes, laugh at yourself, and see what you need to change."

When he arrived at Kemper Military School, Will had to smile, thinking back at what had happened. "I guess it was a pretty silly thing to do, roping my teacher. I'm not going to do that again."

Larry Ett laughed. "Good for you! You're beginning to develop your sense of humor."

Soon, Will had a neat military uniform like the other boys. The students enjoyed Will's humor. As they laughed, some of the boys began to see what was funny in their own lives.

"You're very good at speaking, Will," one teacher told him. "You have a good memory and a quick mind. You're smart and you always make us laugh while giving us something to think about. You win the medal for the best speaker in the school."

Will liked that he was the best speaker, but he still would rather play than work. He didn't spend much time studying most of his subjects, and knew that he wasn't doing well in school.

Will was so unhappy with his grades, that he decided to do something drastic. What do you think it was?

Will ran away from school. He climbed out a window and lowered himself down on his rope. "I'm quitting school," Will said.

"I don't think quitting is a good idea, Will," warned Larry Ett. But Will wasn't listening. He had made up his mind. It was a decision that Will regretted as he got older.

He did not want to face his father, so Will did not go home. Because he was good at roping, he went to a ranch and got a job as a cowboy.

While he was a cowboy, Will got to practice his roping without getting into any trouble. His roping was getting better and better.

But being a cowboy and tending cattle was harder work than he thought. Both Larry Ett and Will were hot and dusty. It was so dusty you couldn't even see Larry Ett!

One day Larry Ett coughed and said, "Why not go home, Will? Even if your father is angry with you, he will be glad to see you."

Both Will and his Dad were glad when Will came home. His Dad was disappointed with Will's behavior, but still loved him a lot.

Larry Ett said, "Running away from school, Will, was sure one of your dumbest ideas. You looked so silly and it's too bad you didn't graduate."

Will smiled and said, "That was pretty dumb."

Larry Ett chuckled. "Well, at least you're smiling at your dumb mistakes. Maybe it will help you learn."

After a while, Will's dad said, "It's good to have you staying at home, Will.

"I hope working as a cowboy has taught you something. I have to be away on important business. While I'm gone, you'll be the boss of the ranch. Make sure everyone does their job, Will."

What kind of boss do you think Will was?

Will wasn't a very good boss. He built a stage on the ranch. He stood on the stage and practiced his rope tricks. He told funny stories and made the cowboys and cowgirls laugh.

Will knew how to make people laugh. But he didn't know the first thing about making them work.

"Oh, no!" cried Will's father when he came back to the ranch. "Will, aren't you ever going to grow up and be responsible?"

"Sorry, Dad," said Will. "I guess I just don't know how to be a ranch boss. I want to do what I'm good at."

So, Will went off to join a rodeo.

Do you know what a rodeo is?

It's a contest where cowhands can win money if they are the best at riding or roping.

At first Will was put into a cowboy band that helped entertain the rodeo customers.

"That's pretty funny," said Larry Ett. "You can't really play a musical instrument."

"It's very funny," Will laughed. Then he held a trombone to his lips and pretended to play it.

You see, the band was getting ready to play a joke on the other cowboys. As you can imagine, with Will's sense of humor, he was looking forward to being a part of it.

The leader of the band called to the rough, tough cowboys who came to ride and rope in the rodeo. "I'll bet I have a cowboy in my band who can rope a calf faster than any of you real cowboys!"

"No way!" laughed the cowboys.

Will, who had been practicing his roping for a long time, thought, "Those cowboys are sure in for a surprise."

The roping contest was held, and who do you think won?

Will won! The funny joke was on the cowboys.

"Hooray! Hooray!" everyone cheered. "Will Rogers is the best calf roper in the whole rodeo!"

"Nice going, Will!" shouted Larry Ett. Will liked roping in the rodeo.

But, every now and then, he also liked to go home.

On one of his trips home, Will met someone special.

There was a new girl in town. Her name was Betty Blake.

"Wow!" thought Will. "She's the prettiest girl I've ever seen. I've got to make her notice me!" He rode his bicycle past Betty's house.

He tried to show off by standing on his head while riding the bike. But Will fell off his bike and hurt himself. He was embarrassed. But then, he laughed.

Can you guess who Will laughed at?

Yes, Will laughed at *himself!* He knew he looked silly. And now he could even laugh at a situation *he* was in.

"Gee," Will thought, "it feels pretty good when I laugh at myself!" Larry Ett was so proud of Will for developing his sense of humor.

Betty laughed too. And what do you think Betty thought about a boy who could laugh at himself when he made a mistake? "I like him!" she said to herself.

Later, Will and Betty began to see a lot of each other. Will thought that one day he might marry Betty. But first, he wanted to travel. Going on a boat to far-off places seemed like a good idea.

But when Will traveled by boat, he got very seasick. "Oooh! I feel terrible!" Will groaned. Larry Ett didn't feel well either.

In time, Will got over being seasick, and he loved boats. He traveled to many faraway places: Europe, South America, Africa and Australia.

Will missed what he could have learned at school, so when he was on a long voyage, he read as many books as he could. And, of course, he practiced his roping.

After a while, Will became a champion roper and people paid money to watch him toss his rope. He had fun traveling, and meeting many different kinds of people. Will realized, "Wherever people are in the world, they are pretty much the same." Will loved many people and they loved him.

When Will finally arrived back in the United States, he did something spectacular. What do you think it was?

It surprised everyone, even Will.

One day, when Will was doing his roping act at a rodeo in New York, a wild steer suddenly broke out of its pen. It crashed through the fence and charged into the audience. People screamed.

"That steer could kill someone!" Will exclaimed. He quickly whirled his rope in the air and threw it around the steer's neck. Will dug his heels into the dirt and pulled the rope with all his might.

The crowd cheered! "He saved us!" they shouted.

Will Rogers was a hero! The next day Will's picture was in the New York newspapers.

Larry Ett said "You're famous. Maybe you could get a job doing your rope tricks on stage. More people will pay money to see you now!"

Will had never thought about the stage before. But do you think it was going to be that easy for Will?

No! Most theater managers thought that rope tricks belonged in a rodeo, but not on a New York stage.

"Sorry," they said to Will. "We can't use you."

It was a difficult time for Will. The rodeo had left town. Will had no job. "I was pretty silly to think I'd get work just because I had my picture in the paper," he said. Then he laughed at himself, and he felt better.

At last, Will persuaded one theater man to give him a chance to perform his rope tricks. He could even take his pony on the stage.

The pony wore special rubber boots so it wouldn't slip and fall. But someone had left whipped cream on the floor of the stage. The pony slid across the stage and almost fell into the audience.

People laughed. "That's pretty funny," said Will. "But I could hurt my pony this way." After that, Will left the pony out of his stage act.

Then one night, when Will was on stage, he made a mistake! He got his rope tangled up around his legs.

Will looked silly and was embarrassed. But he used his sense of humor. He grinned and said, "A rope isn't so bad to get tangled up in — if it isn't around your neck." The audience laughed!

From then on, Will put humor into his roping act, and people enjoyed it more than ever.

Even though many people liked Will, he felt lonely. There was someone special he wanted to be with.

So what do you think he did?

Will went home to see Betty. He asked her to marry him. He was so happy when she said, "Yes!"

And who do you think Will pretended was the best man? It was Larry Ett, who winked and whispered, "This is fun being the best man. I'm glad you and Betty decided to get married."

Later on Will told everybody, "The day I roped Betty, I did the star performance of my life."

After they were married, Will and Betty began to raise a family.

Will went on doing his roping act on the stage. But now, what he said was so funny that people wanted to hear what he would say next.

"I can't keep saying the same things," Will said to Betty. "I need new jokes all the time."

Betty suggested, "Why don't you make jokes about the things you read in the newspapers everyday?"

"What a great idea!" exclaimed Will. "If you could see the funny side of what was in the serious news, it could make you laugh. Might even make you feel better."

He hugged Betty and decided to try out the idea as soon as he could.

"Well, all I know is what I read in the papers," Will would say on stage. He said something funny about what he had read and the audience laughed.

Will was happy. At last, he was doing the thing he really did best. He wasn't just twirling a rope. Will Rogers was using his sense of humor.

And he was becoming a great humorist — someone who can make people laugh, and think!

Will helped his audience see the funny side of what people in the news were doing.

And it helped many of them to look and laugh at the funny things they were doing in their own lives.

The more people laughed, the more they enjoyed themselves.

Will didn't usually get nervous when he did his act. But one night, the theater manager almost had to push him on stage. Will had heard that Woodrow Wilson, the President of the United States, was in the audience!

"Oh, no!" groaned Will. "I was going to tell jokes about the President. Suppose he doesn't have a sense of humor? He may get angry."

Will told his jokes, but people in the audience didn't laugh like they usually did. They were watching the President to see what he did.

Then, President Wilson laughed out loud so hard that he almost fell out of his chair. Everyone else laughed too. They loved seeing such an important person laugh at himself.

Later, after the show was over, the President did something special. What do you suppose he did?

The President of the United States went backstage to shake hands with Will Rogers.

He said, "Good show Will. You reminded me to take my situations seriously, but not take myself too seriously. I can't tell you how long it has been since I've laughed at myself. Thank you."

Larry Ett felt a little shy and hid behind Will. But after the President left, Will thought he heard Larry Ett ask, "Wouldn't your parents be proud of you tonight?" Will smiled as he knew his mom and dad *would* be proud of him!

More and more people wanted to know what Will had to say.

So, Will was invited to be on the radio where many people could hear him in their homes and at work.

He was also asked to write a column for the newspapers.

He was even asked to be in the movies!

Each of these were ways that Will helped people laugh and enjoy their own sense of humor.

It was hard work acting in the movies, but it was fun too. Will was happy.

Will worked hard and got very good at what he was doing — writing for the newspapers, talking on the radio, appearing on stage, and acting in movies.

Sometimes Will would take time out, while making a movie, to write.

Often, he sat on the running board of his car and typed his piece for the newspaper. Larry Ett looked over his shoulder. "You've really developed your sense of humor, Will," he seemed to say.

"Now you're sharing how to see the funny side of things with so many other people."

During a time called The Great Depression, many people had no jobs and no money. Almost everyone worried about what would happen to them.

But, no matter how bad things were in the world, or for Will in his own life, he was smart enough to see the value of looking at the funny side of any situation — even a bad situation.

So, people who were having a difficult time liked to listen to Will.

When they gathered around their radios and listened to Will Rogers, people had to laugh — even about things that usually worried them.

Will's humor helped thousands of people get through some very bad times.

How do you think humor might help you get through some of *your* difficult times?

Everybody felt better when they laughed — even the newly elected President, Calvin Coolidge. Many people knew that he was a serious man who almost never smiled.

Will wasn't sure, however, that he could make Mr. Coolidge smile, let alone laugh.

But, when the new President met and listened to Will Rogers' sense of humor, even he laughed and enjoyed himself.

Will Rogers met lots of famous people, including kings and queens and heads of state. They all enjoyed him and learned from his sense of humor.

But there were other people Will liked to be with just as much.

Will enjoyed meeting people who lived in small towns around the world. He got the ideas for some of his best jokes when he listened carefully to what the people were saying.

But more than any other place, Will liked to be home on his ranch with his wife and children.

Will liked to sit outside with Betty and watch their children. They were learning to rope — something Will enjoyed doing all his life.

Will remembered back to when he was a child. He thought, "It sure was fun to pretend my rope was really Larry Ett. I learned so much from just listening to myself."

Then Larry Ett seemed to say, "Will, you and I know that you have done this yourself. I was just made up from your imagination. It is now time for me to be on my way."

Will smiled and said, "I know. Thank you. Thank you so much!"

"You're welcome," said Larry Ett, and then he began to disappear.

Will felt peaceful and happy. But life on his ranch was not always so peaceful and quiet for Will.

All kinds of people liked to come to Will's ranch and visit him. He had lots of friends.

Do you know why so many people liked to be with Will Rogers?

Yes, they liked Will because he had a good sense of humor. When they were with him, they laughed more and enjoyed themselves!

Will liked everyone. In fact, Will Rogers once said, "I never met a man I didn't like." Will was happy, and so the people around him were happy when they were with him.

And now, as our story nears its end, what do *you* think?

What you may want to do in your own life may be very different from what Will Rogers wanted to do.

You can choose what you want for yourself.

Whatever you choose, you may find that when you have a sense of humor and are smart enough to laugh at what is funny in a situation, in big and small ways, you can be happier too — just like our friend, Will Rogers.

Then perhaps, you can have fun making the world a little better place — by sharing what you have learned with others!

The End

ValueTales®
DISCUSSION

Now that you know about *The Value of Humor: The Tale of Will Rogers* —

What do *you* think?

 What did you like most about the story?

 What did Will like to practice doing?

 What do you think would have happened if Will Rogers did not have a sense of humor?

 How do *you* feel when *you* have a sense of humor?

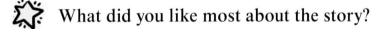 How could you use *The Value of Humor*, in big and little ways, in your own life?

HISTORICAL FACTS
Will Rogers
1879-1935

William Penn Adair Rogers, the youngest of eight children, was born on November 4, 1879, in his parents' ranch house halfway between the towns of Claremore and Oolagah in what was the Indian territory and is now the state of Oklahoma.

His father Clem was one-eighth Cherokee and his mother Mary, one-quarter Cherokee, which Will figured made him about "one-eighth cigar-store Injun."

Even the name of the state where he was born, Oklahoma, was derived from Indian words. (*Okla* means red and *homma* means people.) Will later said, "My ancestors didn't come over on the *Mayflower*. They met the boat."

Will's mother died when he was only ten years old. It was a great loss to Will, who missed her gentle manner, her sense of humor, love of music, and easy way with people — some of the strongest traits inherited by her son.

The fun-loving son of a prosperous father, Will had every chance for a good education. But as bright as he was, Will wasn't interested in any of the many different schools he attended.

Will Rogers always spoke with a distinct Western drawl and a total disregard for proper English. When Will is quoted in this book, his words are paraphrased into language which most people feel is more appropriate for children to learn. His wife tried to encourage Will to speak properly, but Will always felt that his drawl was at least partially responsible for his unique success.

More than anything else though, it was Will's sense of humor that helped him succeed as philosopher, columnist, movie star, radio personality, philanthropist, and human being.

In 1899, Will met Betty Blake. They were married nine years later in Betty's hometown of Rogers, Arkansas. Betty was a great part of Will's life — his best critic, his financial and business manager, his partner, and his favorite person. Will and Betty had four children, but to their sorrow, one of their sons, Fred, died in infancy. Their three surviving children, Will, Jr., Jimmy, and Mary, were an important part of their lives.

In 1905, Will met a fellow rodeo performer, Tom Mix, who talked of his travels to far-off China, and his days with Teddy Roosevelt's Rough Riders. These conversations kindled Will's desire to travel. And when Will wasn't at home with his family, he was usually traveling. He was a great promoter of two new modes of transportation: the automobile and the airplane. His friends included Henry Ford (who presented Will with the first Model A car) and most of the leading aviators of his time, including Billy Mitchell, Charles Lindbergh, and Wiley Post.

Will's life ended in 1935 on a flight around the world with Wiley Post. Their plane crashed in desolate Point Barrow, Alaska. The entire world mourned his death.

It was very risky to fly in those days. The airplane was just being developed. But Will had always been one to take risks. He once gave a friend the advice, "Go out on a limb. That's where the fruit is."

Will took a chance when he poked fun at hypocrisy, smugness, and greed — even if they occurred in the most famous and important people. He did so with a good sense of humor, however. And people from every level of society loved him for it.

It is ironic that it was the humorist Will Rogers who said, "You can judge a man's greatness by how much he is missed."

ENJOY THE ENTIRE VALUETALES® SERIES!

1	2	3	4	5	6	7	8	9	10	11	12	13	14	15	16	17	18	19	20	21	22	23	24
BELIEVING IN YOURSELF	HONESTY	FAIRNESS	COURAGE	SHARING	HUMOR	LEARNING	HELPING	UNDERSTANDING	PATIENCE	RESPECT	FRIENDSHIP	CURIOSITY	DEDICATION	CARING	RESPONSIBILITY	SAVING	KINDNESS	CREATIVITY	TRUTH AND TRUST	IMAGINATION	FORESIGHT	DETERMINATION	GIVING
PASTEUR	CONFUCIUS	BLY	ROBINSON	MAYO BROTHERS	ROGERS	CURIE	TUBMAN	MEAD	WRIGHT BROTHERS	LINCOLN	ADDAMS	COLUMBUS	SCHWEITZER	ROOSEVELT	BUNCHE	FRANKLIN	FRY	EDISON	COCHISE	DICKENS	JEFFERSON	KELLER	BEETHOVEN

VALUETALES® SUBSCRIPTION
TIMELESS VALUES DELIVERED MONTHLY!

You can provide children with a new ValueTales® book each month with your
ValueTales® subscription. $16.^{95}/month + s&h

Phone 1-800-515-0848

Visit www.ValueTales.com